Cat Spelled Backwards Doesn't Spell God.

The Dogs of Portland by Jeff Selis

First published 1998 by Wieden & Kennedy, Inc.

Published, printed and bound in Portland, Oregon.
Set in Trade Gothic.
Designed by E. Hawthorne Hunt.

Inquiries to the publisher should be addressed to:

Bill Davenport
Managing Director
Wieden & Kennedy
320 S.W. Washington
Portland, Or. 97204
(503) 820.2600

Library of Congress Catalog Number: 98-96758
ISBN: 0-9668361-0-3

The only reason this book exists is because of a generous grant from Wieden & Kennedy, Inc. — an advertising agency in Portland, Oregon. I was awarded the grant after entering my idea into Wieden & Kennedy's first Slime Mold Award. This award was designed to encourage employees to realize their creative potential in any medium. My idea was to publish a book on dogs — a book of photographs and stories that would convey the uniqueness and importance of dogs, with proceeds benefiting the Oregon Humane Society.

The dogs in these pages were selected mostly by chance. I would see one dog in a park, or another on a walk. One proud owner would give me a tip on another — and so on and so on. One weekend I went to Portland's annual Doggie Dash. I found lots of great dogs there. It was my intention to find dogs from all over the city. I think I've done a good job of that, though I'm a bit partial to Northeast.

I photographed each dog with my 1965 Polaroid Land Camera 180. You may notice some imperfections with the photographs, such as emulsion spots from the separation of the photo and negative. I like these imperfections. I think they add character and reality to the shots. After all, my goal was not to produce the perfect print, but to capture the true personality of each dog.

Anyway, I had a blast making this book. I cherished every drop of drool on my clothes, every lick on my cheek and every nose print on my lens.

Many thanks to Wieden & Kennedy for throwing me such a huge bone.

— Jeff Selis

This book is dedicated to my mom and her dog, Max.

Thank you, Mom, for getting me over my fear of dogs by bringing home our first dog, Whiz. And thank you for always going back on your word after saying, "Never another dog!" In my life, I'll never be without one.

I'll miss you forever, Mom. May you and Max rest in peace.

I love you.

Your son, Jeff

Buddha

Buddha gets his belly rubs in the heights of Southwest Portland's Council Crest.

He has a deep affection for watermelon, corn chips and raisins. If he finds himself getting a little too soft in the middle, he will head out to do some serious trail running or take to the mountain for some cross-country skiing.

Buddha is two years old and has yet to find the humor in the noise that his owner makes through the empty paper towel tube.

Little Bit

Little Bit enjoys nothing more than hanging out on her master's lap in Northwest Portland.

She is a purebred dachshund who hates being called a wiener dog.

Gus

The thing Gus hates the most is being hosed down, but
that doesn't keep him from doing what he loves to do
most — roll around in the neighbor's compost pile. P-U!

Gus is a neighborhood favorite up on the Alameda
Ridge in Northeast Portland.

El Toro De Las Nubes

You can call him Tor.

Being the runt of the litter has never stopped Tor from being a social butterfly. He loves company, and he'll lend an ear to anything except country music.

Tor graces the area of Beaumont Village in Northeast Portland.

Katie

Katie resides in the Parkrose district of Northeast Portland.
She loves to spin around on her hind legs for Crunchy Corn Bran
cereal and get her nails painted every trip to the beauty parlor.

Katie will sit in her "pouting chair" whenever she is left behind.

Charlie

What floats Charlie's boat is when his mom comes home from her job in Northwest Portland and takes him on a long run.

He's not your stereotypical Doberman — the one thing Charlie can't live without is his binky. That's right, his binky.

Still, one would be wise to think twice before testing him.

Jack

Jack takes flight in the Grant Park area of Northeast Portland. He loves chasing and fetching, and fancies cat poop when the litter box hasn't been cleaned.

Although he's a very lovable pup, Jack has a running feud with German shepherds. They seem to like to pick on dogs with lots of spots.

Cy

Cy was named after the legendary pitcher. While he never could have hit a Cy Young fastball, he definitely could have gone to bat with him in a cookie-eating contest. Cy loves a cookie.

Cy's home field is in Southeast Portland.

Alexander and Joshua

Alexander and Joshua love kids. Lucky for these two, their Northeast Portland home is full of them. They love it when the kids take them on long walks through the neighborhood. When the kids aren't around they are content to just lie in the shade.

Alexander has six toes on one of his back paws.

Brenainn

Brenainn is an Irish wolfhound who was born in Dublin, and has lived in Portland since 1992. Though his accent isn't as thick as it used to be, Brenainn upholds his Irish tradition by marching in the St. Patrick's Day Parade every March. It is by far his favorite day of the year.

Brenainn opposes war, fleas and pills.

Romeo

Forget Juliet, the only thing this Romeo would die for is a fresh-baked cookie.

Romeo is a Great Dane puppy who is still learning as he goes. For instance, whenever he sees another dog on television, Romeo will walk behind the TV set in search of this four-legged stranger.

Romeo lounges in his Northeast Portland home where he will only drink water from the sink.

Riley

The life of Riley must consist of a daily dose of fruits and vegetables. He *loves* his fruits and veggies. If only kids could be more like Riley!

Riley also likes to ride in the car, unless of course it's a trip to the groomer. Other than the vacuum cleaner, there's nothing he despises more than being bathed and brushed.

Riley has been hiding out in the West Slope area of Southwest Portland for almost four years now.

Otis

Everyone calls him a pit bull, but Otis is really a purebred Staffordshire bull terrier who's probably the friendliest dog you will ever meet. The only way he would kill you is by licking you to death.

Otis loves any kind of movement, whether it's pacing around the living room furniture with his favorite toy, or taking a hike through Forest Park on the weekend.

The only thing Otis hates is when his parents have to go to work.

Bart

Hide the varmints, because Bart is a full-on terrier and he loves a good chase. One time Bart's parents brought him to a Thanksgiving dinner but no one told him that the host's pet rat "Rocket" wasn't on the menu.

Oops.

Bart is fenced up in Southeast Portland.

Ellie

Ellie is a product of the Greyhound Placement Association of Portland. Having spent her early years at the track, Ellie retired and found a cozy home in Northeast Portland. An unfortunate accident at the age of seven cost Ellie a leg, but she never lost her spirit. Ellie now spends much of her time visiting patients in nursing homes.

For kicks, she likes to hang out at the playground where she'll still take on anyone in the hundred-yard dash.

Ellie is now nine years old. 63 for you and me.

Hoover

Hoover marks his territory on Dogwood Lane in Southwest Portland. However, city life comes second for this dog who relishes every chance he gets to go chukar-hunting with his mom and dad in the wide-open country.

Kramer

Kramer is the lovable protector of a Northeast Portland family of four. His favorite thing to do is stand guard at his mom's big bay window overlooking their street.

Kramer is such a good protector that he once thwarted a robbery attempt on his mom in the parking lot of the area grocery store. He then cornered the bad guy until someone with two legs came and took him away.

This dog deserves a medal.

Phoebe Snow

Phoebe Snow has been white-water rafting and survived a
swim down a class-4 rapid. Want more? She will sing for beer.

She is a popular sight on Hawthorne Boulevard where she goes
to work with her mom five days a week.

Phoebe Snow is easily annoyed by people with high-pitched
voices who try to pick her up.

Lucy

According to Lucy's owner, she is the best dog that has ever lived. Her owner also adds that when people climb into his truck they say "P-U!," but he doesn't smell anything.

Lucy loves doing tricks for treats and hanging out at Wilshire Park in Northeast Portland.

Her pet peeve is going potty on wet grass.

Choco

Choco is a friendly guard dog who protects his family's home on Northeast 14th Street. Prowlers beware, he may not see you coming, but he will definitely smell you. And you don't want that.

By the way, Choco has his fair share of 1st-place show ribbons. It's a hobby when he's off duty.

Shawnee

Shawnee loves people, kitties and back rubs.

She takes a walk with her mom every night up and down Dunckley Street in Northeast Portland.

Spunky as ever, she's 84 going on 13.

Norman

A stray, Norman was window-shopping for a home one day in Southeast Portland.

Norman is now in charge of security at his mother's shop on 13th Street in Sellwood. Norman greets paying customers with a smile and a wag of the tail.

Friedrick

Friedrick is a Weimaraner who loves to climb rocks and trees. Weimaraners have large feet with which they can clutch things.

Friedrick's favorite thing to clutch is his momma. She's the one who provides him shelter in the Mount Tabor area of Southeast Portland.

Bogey

Bogey's four favorite words are *chicken-basted rawhide bone*. He will clean his teeth on one for hours. Say the word bath, however, and this dog will high-tail it the other way.

Bogey found his way to the Portland area via the Humane Society in Las Vegas. His owners spotted him there and decided to take the gamble. Eight years later, he's proved to be a pretty safe bet.

Double Bogey

Anna

Anna is the pride and joy of her doting owner. The two of them share a loft in Northwest Portland's Pearl District. Anna goes everywhere her master goes — whether it's to work, to the beach, to the store or to bed.

She's showered with praise, attention and gifts; every lady should be so lucky.

Brandy

Brandy is following in some pretty impressive footsteps. The two poodles before him, Jocho and Beau, lived to the ripe old ages of 15 and 14, respectively.

One of his favorite activities is frolicking in the trout pond at his master's Sylvan Heights estate in Southwest Portland — leaving the fish alone, of course.

Brandy's unique coloring made for a difficult choice of a name. The alternate was Cognac. Either way, he's definitely a dog worth toasting.

Here's to your health, Brandy.

Caesar and Sammy

Caesar and Sammy have got it made in the shade. They live on three acres
in the West Hills of Portland. They get all the exercise they need chasing each
other around the grounds of their sprawling estate.

When the sun comes out and Caesar spots his shadow he will drop everything
simply to stare at it until the clouds roll in.

Lucky they don't live in Southern California.

Lucy D

Lucy D gets wiped out playing games with her big brother and big sister
in the big yard of their big house off Skyline Boulevard in Northwest Portland.

Rest and relaxation is her big reward until it's time to go again.

Baby

A trip to the nearest park is a pretty sweet deal, but there's nothing Baby loves more than eating hot dogs and watching TV.

Baby is two years old and does her channel surfing in the Sullivan's Gulch area of Northeast Portland.

Spot

Spot's favorite pastime is chasing her tail. The only sight crazier than Spot chasing her tail is her reaction to the recycling truck when it pulls up to her Northeast Portland home on Monday mornings. She absolutely loses it!

Spot is a product of the Bull Terrier Rescue League, and is now a happy and almost sane nine years old.

Chuck

Chuck's favorite activities all revolve around water. He loves sailing, fishing and swimming. Heck, he's ecstatic if he gets sprayed down with the garden hose.

Chuck loves all people, animals and insects. His master says he wouldn't even hurt a flea. Crazy dog!

Chuck soils his turf in the Kenton area of North Portland.

Barkley

With enough hugs and kisses for the entire city of Portland, Barkley's overflowing affection still wasn't enough to keep his first owner from abandoning him in an orchard.

Barkley was rescued, however, and provided a home near Westmoreland Park in Southeast Portland.

He continues to love everyone — except the vet.

Basia

Basia loves her mommas the most. She also loves back scratches and sniffing around Sacajawea Park in Northeast Portland.

Basia is seven years old and has yet to learn to walk on linoleum floors.

Micho pronounced "Mee-ko"

Micho is a white German shepherd who gets her daily exercise fetching balls, rocks and sticks in the back of her parents' two-acre home near Powell Butte in Southeast Portland. In fact, she will retrieve anything you throw her — except grapes.

Micho is three years old and loves to snack on "kitty roca."

Titan

He may be the neighborhood bulldog, but he's no neighborhood bully.
Titan is the most popular dog on Northwest 23rd Avenue.

The only thing he loves more than your attention is vanilla ice cream.
It's his reward for being good.

If only we could all have such incentive.

Rocky

Quite the knockout, Rocky gets his daily workout along the ridge above Oaks Park near his home in Southeast Portland.

Rocky is in his second year and loves to 'KO' spiders with his long, pink tongue.

Sydney

New to Northeast Portland, Sydney is a puppy who loves anything that's not hooked to the ground. This includes her momma's new Nikes, dirty underwear and sweaty socks.

Sydney also loves to pick strawberries and raspberries off the vine.

At her young age, the only thing she doesn't like is reading the daily newspaper. She poops on it instead.

Callie

Callie loves her human sister Jenny who suffers from epilepsy.
She gives her the love she needs every day in Northeast Portland.

Callie is especially excited about the family's new lake house
just 60 minutes out of town — a place to rest and relax and fetch
the balls thrown into the lake by Jenny.

You're a good dog, Callie.

Paddy

Paddy shares a bed with her mom in the Cedar Hills area of Southwest Portland. Her favorite treat is a cherry tomato. She actually has her own tomato plant in the garden that she harvests on her own every summer.

Paddy wakes at the crack of dawn each morning so she can get an early start chasing squirrels. She has yet to catch one, but Paddy is determined to succeed before her dog days are over.

Binky

Binky loves Bongo.

Bongo

Bongo loves Binky.

Kersey, Porter and Buck

Kersey, Porter and Buck are the pillars of 22nd Avenue in Northeast Portland.
They are the true definition of Neighborhood Watch. The only time they let down
their guard is during the annual 22nd Avenue Block Party — they won't claim
responsibility for their funny-looking humans dancing in the middle of the street.

Kersey, Porter and Buck were named after three favorite Trail Blazers. If only
they had a brother named Jordan.

Giani

Giani's mom keeps a bamboo fountain in the sunroom of their Northeast Portland home. When Mom's not around, Giani loves to duck her head under the water and remove the rocks, one by one. Then she hides them around the house. When the rocks are gone she takes a seat in the fountain as if it were her own personal spa. Then Mom replaces the rocks, and the process starts all over again.

Giani was named after a comet discovered by Carl Sagan.

Sherlock

Sherlock is a black and tan coonhound mix who has many of the same attributes as the master detective himself. Whether it's a raccoon, an opossum, or a bone buried long ago he is always searching to solve a mystery.

Sherlock is ten years old and digs up clues in the hills of Southwest Portland.

Boo Radley

Boo Radley likes everyone and everything, which is amazing since he'd been abandoned twice before the age of six months. If you give him some food you've got a friend for life. His expression at the dinner table says, "Are you going to eat that?"

Boo Radley is now four years old and has a home forever in Historic Irvington.

Chelsea

Chelsea was born in New York where she lived with a family that was busting out at the seams. Something had to give. Chelsea was the odd one out. Fate took over and Chelsea waved goodbye to her family and the asphalt jungle and made her way to the lush and green Great Northwest.

Chelsea now enjoys car rides in the country, long walks in the park, and just kicking back to the cool sounds of old Dean Martin.

Seems Chelsea never had it so good.

Geronimo

Call him Joe for short but, please, don't call him short. Joe has
a serious little man's complex.

Joe got his full name after perching himself on his mom's window
ledge five stories above a downtown Portland street. Had Joe not
been coerced back in with a tasty treat, no one knows just how far
he would have gone to prove his doghood.

King

King, formally known as "CH. TLC's King of Hearts V Breaker," is a prized show dog from the outskirts of Southeast Portland. King loves to travel the region and strut his stuff.

He can't stand the heat, but he loves to be in the kitchen, especially when there are fresh-baked goodies around.

King is four years old and weighs a mere 205 pounds.

Big Daddy

If Big Daddy were to run an ad in the doggie personals it would read:

*Charming, self-absorbed, sexy male seeks companion who loves
giving affection and snacking on pigs' ears. Should cherish walks in
the park and have lots of patience for a marker's mentality.
Sucker for Italian greyhounds.*

The legend of Big Daddy lives on at Wallace Park in Northwest Portland.

Molson

Molson is golden. He is the resident dog at Southwest Portland's Hopewell House — a hospice facility for people with life-threatening illnesses.

Molson will go from one room to the next spending quality time with any patient who wants or needs it. Molson has quite a bit of insight into what patients are going through. He had cancer himself, even had chemotherapy and lost his hair for a while.

He must be an angel.

Barley

Only about two inches off the ground when standing on all fours, Barley becomes "Air Barley" when his mom takes him to Laurelhurst Park to throw around the Frisbee. After a game of fetch he likes to cool his belly in the nearest mud puddle.

Barley is two years old and can't stand having his nails clipped.

"Vedorrie!"

When Vedorrie's not relaxing around her stately home off of Vista Avenue in Southwest Portland, she's probably out traveling the globe. She's been to Brazil, France, Italy and Holland.

Her favorite airline is KLM because the flight attendants get a kick out of speaking her name. In Dutch, Vedorrie means "Damn it!"

Vedorrie's favorite meal is waffles.

Woody and Rosie

Woody and Rosie love to hang out in Washington Park, but be careful if you're having a picnic nearby because they won't hesitate to invite themselves over.

These littermates are love sponges constantly seeking attention. They share a queen-sized bed with their humans.

Timmie, Sophie, Lucy, Charlie, Frazier, Otis & Maggie May

These siblings were all taken in and nursed back to health by one amazing woman. Otis was abandoned in Estacada, Frazier was tied to a picnic table in MacLeay Park and Timmie was left in Battleground. Charlie lost his master to AIDS. One way or another, they were all in need of some serious TLC.

All are thriving now in their mother's pet shop on Northwest Vaughn Street. There they await the day a permanent owner will come and take them home, but if the right person doesn't come along, they've got a pretty sweet deal just where they are.

Oscar

Oscar is a Humane Society rescue. He will drool over anything good that comes his way, whether it's his nightly walk around his Northeast Portland neighborhood, or a table scrap from his big brother Matt.

Oscar is a lucky seven years old.

Bleu

Bleu's favorite thing to do is watch people eat. He figures if he stares long enough he's going to win out. The only thing Bleu won't eat is parsley. Go figure.

Bleu misses his companion Max very much. What he misses most is licking the goobers away from Max's eyes first thing in the morning.